SECRETS OF GOD'S CHAMPIONS

Olukayode Agbeyomi

Library of Congress Control Number: 2018675309
Printed in the United States of America

*To my remarkable family; my beautiful wife,
Pastor Feyi Agbeyomi, and my three wonderful
children: Glory, David, and Toyan. And, to the
champions of God prospering worldwide.*

CONTENTS

INTRODUCTION

God's champions belong to a kingdom that is not from here. Just like every kingdom has its own culture and language, likewise God's kingdom has its culture and language. Each door has a particular key, that no other key will be capable of opening. When God's people learn to use the right keys, they begin to operate as champions of God. There is no battle they can't win. God is depending on them and is in search of champions that are yet to discover that they carry the seed of 'stars'. I have seen God reveal champions in all the places around the world that I have been privileged to minister at. The power of the Holy Spirit falls upon these people during the ministration, and the seed of champions begins to germinate in them. The Holy Spirit then takes them through varied kingdom experiences until the champion within them is born.

When Prophet Elijah was running away because Jezebel placed a prize on his head, the prophet thought he was the only servant of God left that had not bowed to Baal. God told Elijah that there were seven thousand other prophets who had never bowed to Baal. Every believer has the potential to be a champion of God. It all depends on choice. There is a champion in you. May your choices not cost you to live in the shadow of your true self. Operating in the right atmosphere is key to the emergence of champions.

Many champions are buried without emerging or reaching their full potential. You will emerge a champion in your generation in Jesus name. Champions are Christ's ambassadors that represent His kingdom here on earth.

"I have heard a rumour from the Lord, and an ambassador is sent unto the heathen, saying, Gather ye together, and come against her, and rise up to the battle."
Jeremiah 49:14

Ambassadors are spokesmen of the Lord, and they are to make clear and distinct sounds in order to prevent confusion. Except the trumpet makes a distinct sound, who shall be ready for battle? (1 Corinthians 14:8)

"For which I am an ambassador in bonds: that therein I may speak boldly, as I ought to speak." Ephesians 6:20

Paul revealed that he himself is an ambassador of God's kingdom. An ambassador is a representative of a kingdom. When an ambassador speaks, it is as if the head of the kingdom has spoken. An ambassador is expected to know and speak his kingdom's language. It is forbidden to have an ambassador that cannot speak his kingdom's language. Paul revealed his boldness to speak about his assignment as an ambassador. Receive the boldness that will provoke you into your destiny as a champion today, and I declare that the fire of the Holy Spirit will consume everything holding your destiny captive in Jesus name. Enter into that liberty wherewith the Holy Spirit has made you free and begin to do as occasion serves you. It is your turn.

CHAPTER 1

Emergence of a Champion

Champions are usually revealed by God. Situations sometimes initiate the release of God's champion. Elijah was revealed as a champion, after refusing to worship the idol Baal, and staying true to the one and only God. David was revealed by the harassment of God's people by Goliath, Gideon by incessant raids of Israel by the Midianites, Joseph by famine, and Moses by the enslavement of God's people in Egypt. One issue necessitates the release, and the aim is to draw the people back to God.

Needs are vital in the release of God's champions. Champions are released as answers to the predicament of God's people. Clearly put, troubles, problems, and chaos are all tools that God uses to release champions into the world. It is imperative to clarify that God is not an author of confusion, and does not tempt any one with evil (James 1:13). After this introduction, problems may be seen as something that God takes advantage of to bless His people. Problems are unsolved issues and require solutions from anyone bold, innovative and sometimes sporadic. Problems are the opportunities created for someone to provide solutions. One opportunity is all it takes to schedule the release of a champion. Opportunity is the door into the season of emergence of the champion.

God is our first champion, and He is the solution to all problems. God previously revealed Himself in eight redemptive names according to man's needs:
1) To the sick, He is Jehovah Rapha; the Lord that heals. (Exodus 15:22-26)
2) In time of need, He is Jehovah Jireh; the Lord that provides. (Genesis 22:12-14)
3) In warfare, He is Jehovah Nissi; the Lord our banner. (Exodus 17:15-16)
4) God is Jehovah Shalom; our peace in times of trouble. (Judges 6:24)
5) Jehovah Raah; our shepherd. (Psalm 23:1)
6) Jehovah-Tsid-Kenu; the Lord our righteousness. (Jeremiah 33:16)
7) Jehovah Sabaoth; the Lord of Host, our protector. (Ps 46:7)
8) Jehovah Shammah; the Lord with us everywhere, omnipresent. (Revelation 21:3)

"My brethren, count it all joy when ye fall into divers' temptations; knowing this, that the trying of your faith worketh patience. But let patience have her perfect work, that ye may be perfect and entire, wanting nothing."

James 1:2-4

CHAPTER 2

There is a Price to Pay

Being a champion requires a prize. Even though the gift of salvation is a free gift, reigning as a champion has a price tag attached to it. To Joshua, it was the Word of God he needed to release the champion in him. The Word of God has a character and integrity. It will not return void to God, until it has accompanied every purpose for which it was sent. God's Word is dependable and never fails. God's Word is the same yesterday, today and forever. God wanted Joshua to know and have His Word so Joshua could speak like God and get God's kind of results. God said to Joshua:

"This book of the law must not depart out of thy mouth but thou shall meditate therein day and night and thou Mayest observe to do according to all that is written therein: for then shall maketh thy way prosperous,
and then thou shall have good success."

Joshua 1:8

Winners are not made in the open; they are secretly baked. God will take his champions through life experiences that will turn them on to God and off to the world.

"I will make a man more precious than fine gold; even a man than the golden wedge of Ophir."

Isaiah 13:12

God always wants to bring out the best in His choice servants. The experience may not be sweet and often one may wonder, "Has God forgotten me? Has God abandoned me? Why am I going through this situation?" Kathryn Kuhlman after passing through tough times once said, "I can take you to the very spot I died." She was known as the friend of the Holy Spirit, and God mightily used her in the healing ministry. For some champions, there is a need to die to self so that the glory of God can rise upon them to shine (Isaiah 60:1).

"I am crucified with Christ: nevertheless I live; yet not I but Christ liveth in me: and the life I now live in the flesh I live by the faith of the son of God, who loved me, and gave himself for me."

Galatians 2:20

Moses was banished from Egypt into the wilderness for forty years, before he could become qualified as God's champion to lead His people. Many champions today can only emerge when they die to self. There is a champion in every believer trying to find expression. Paying the ultimate prize releases you to your destiny.

CHAPTER 3

Champions are Focused

The throne is the direction; the crown is the goal. A focused man is a visionary. Every believer has a champion locked in him or her desiring expression. A focused man imagines the future and gazes constantly on how to get there.

"And the Lord answered me, and said write the vision, and make it plain upon tables, that he may run that readeth it."
Habakkuk 2:2

The vision is clear to the focused man, and he will not be distracted by anything because he is out to achieve his goals and objectives. Visionaries don't quit. Every time a champion gets committed to a course, he always finishes it.

"Rejoice not against me, O my enemy: when I fall, I shall arise; when I sit in darkness, the Lord shall be a light unto me."
Micah 7:8

Until you discover the champion in you, winning will be a mirage.

"Looking onto Jesus the author and finisher of our faith..."
Hebrew 12: 2

Jesus is the author of our faith and He will see to it that your faith is rewarded if you do not doubt. To "look onto" means to depend on; to see Him as your source. To be a champion implies that there is zero tolerance for distraction. Distraction creates a wrong attraction to a different direction.

Distraction refocuses the champion to attend to his "new wrong" attention. Whosoever heaven has approved will surely be great. You are next in line. Great men are pulled down by distraction. Distraction could show up any time and at any place. Distraction pushes a person's focus to energy wasting endeavors while leaving the real job undone. It's a destiny delayer. Great men have fallen for allowing a little distraction into their lives. Even David the sweet psalmist was also caught in the web, but he rose out of it.

"And it came to pass, after the year was expired, at the time when kings go forth to battle, that David sent Joab, and his servants with him, and all Israel; and they destroyed the children of Ammon, and besieged Rabbah, But David tarried still at Jerusalem. And it came to pass in an evening tide that David arose from off his bed, and walked upon the roof of the king's house: and from the roof he saw a woman washing herself; and the woman was very beautiful to look upon." 2 Samuel 11:1

David was playing lazy. He was in bed till evening, and the distraction came as soon as he got out of bed; in form of a woman who was very beautiful to look upon. The flesh kicked in and then the lust of the eyes. David was overtaken by covetousness that led to adultery, and murder of Uriah the husband of Bathsheba. David later married her, but the thing that David did displeased the Lord (2 Samuel 11:27). The effect of that distraction was an unnecessary curse:

"Now therefore, the sword shall never depart from thine house; because thou hast despised me, and has taken the wife of Uriah the Hittite to be thy wife."

2 Samuel 12:8

David despised the Lord when he gave in to distraction. Distraction can be costly, and God may not take it lightly with his champions. Champions, beware of distractions that create a wrong attention for your desire. Check your appetite, if your tongue causes you to err, seek for help and deal with it. God is a just God.

"Howbeit, because by this deed thou hast given great occasion to the enemies of the Lord to blaspheme, the child also that is born unto thee shall surely die."

2 Samuel 12:14

God will never allow His name to be blasphemed by the enemy. Balaam the prophet was invited by Balak, king of Moab to curse the people of Israel, and God was angry with the prophet. Balaam almost got killed by the angel of the Lord.

"Then the Lord opened the eyes of Balaam, and he saw the angel of the Lord standing in the way, and his sword drawn in his hand: and he bowed down his head, and fell flat on his face. And the angel of the Lord said unto him, wherefore hast thou smitten thine ass these three times? Behold, I went out to withstand thee, because thy way is perverse before me: And the ass saw me, and turned from me these three times: unless

she had turned from me, surely now also I had slain thee, and saved her alive." Numbers 22:31-33

Champions do not walk against God's counsel rather in line with God's will and counsel. To do otherwise may be costly. Let everyone who claims to know God depart from iniquity. If you do not stand for God, you will end up being tossed around by every wind of life. Moses the meekest man also got carried away by the occasion and never made it to the promise land. However, when champions fall, they can rise again. David, the sweet psalmist rose. You will rise in Jesus name.

Champions Cannot Marry Just Anyone
Samson is another example of a champion to learn from. Samson decided to pick a wife from the camp of the enemy. It is pertinent to say it is very risky to marry any believer simply because the person is a believer. God is still the Lord of the marriage. He introduced marriage, and He still connects couples to one another. Simply put, champions cannot marry just anybody whether believer or non-believer. Marrying the wrong person can deprive a champion of the destiny to emerge. There is that person that God has prepared for every believer called the "help mate". Marrying the wrong person may be at the price of emerging. Although, the person will make
it to heaven, it may just be another destiny that was not realized as it got buried by wrong desires. Don't get me wrong, God works in mysterious ways and He can link people together as He desires. I once heard of a brother destined to go to a mission field for the Lord but became unqualified for marrying a wrong Christian lady and ended up telling his stories as a trainer of believers going to the mission field. This is not to mock anyone but for the

generation of champions coming to learn from and avoid making the same mistake.

"And Samson went down to Timnath, and saw a woman in Timnath of the daughters of the Philistines. And he came up, and told his father and mother, and said, I have seen a woman in Timnath of the daughter of the Philistines now therefore get her for me for wife." Judges 14:1-2

Despite all warnings from his parents, Samson insisted, saying "get her for me; for she pleases me well" (Judges 14:3). Marriage was never man's idea. How come many seek partners that please them rather than partners that please God for them to fulfill their destiny? A help mate is not only for grocery shopping or bringing children into the world but also to help a man or woman of God emerge as a champion in his or her God-given destiny. The devil has used this aspect to deprive many of their qualifications for God's will for their lives. Champions must always seek the will of God at all times. The will of God will bring you peace and it is important to say that both parties need to prayerfully seek their life partners early so that they don't miss it. One thing every champion should learn is how to hear God's voice. God usually will not speak to you about a life partner in a way he hasn't spoken to you before. If you are not sure, always ask for confirmation and God will confirm it again.

CHAPTER 4

Champions hear God's voice

Champions are not isolated. They hear God's voice and fellowship with
Him. Jesus said:

"My sheep hear my voice and I know them and they follow me."
John 10:27

God always speaks to the ear that wants to hear. There are different ways God speak to believers:

Word of God
This is the most fundamental and dependable way that God uses to speak to his people (Isaiah 55:11). The Word of God is reliable and serves as the basis for other ways by which God speaks to man. The Word of God is quick and powerful, sharper than any two-edged sword (Hebrew 4:12), and the Word of God is written by inspiration.

"All scripture is given by inspiration of God and is profitable for doctrine, for reproof, for correction, for instruction in righteousness." 2 Timothy 3:16–17

If any of the other methods of hearing God's voice contradicts the Word of God, discard it because it is most likely not from God. God will never contradict himself. For example, if someone says he heard God's voice saying he should jump down from the 10th floor. Of course, he might have heard the voice, but it's not God's voice. That person is probably schizophrenic. God won't ask you to commit suicide.

The written Word of God is the Logo called the Bible or the Rhema Word which is the activated (made alive) Logos. The Rhema is the Scripture that jumps out and strikes you when you open the Bible. Logos can also become Rhema through constant reading and meditating on the Logos. Rhema word is formed at the point the Scripture 'opens up and comes alive' giving revelation and enhancing understanding. This Rhema Word is the one that gives miracles to sick folks who are standing on healing Scriptures and others using the Word to meet their needs.

Still Small Voice

This refers to the voice of the Spirit and is best heard early in the morning in a young believer before the beginning of daily activities.

"The spirit of man is the candle of the Lord, searching all the inward parts of the belly." Proverbs 20:27

The regenerated human spirit is connected back to God through the Holy Spirit.

.

Intuition/Inner Witness

This is best described as the ability to 'know' or 'perceive', and it is well developed in women. There may be no logical explanation than 'I just know'. Paul warned in Acts 27:10:

"And said on to them, sir, I perceive that this voyage will be with hurt and much damage, not only of the lading and ship, but also of our lives."

God's Audible Voice

This is God's voice spoken to man. God voice has characteristics:

i) It is authoritative
ii) It does not argue
iii) It's instruction is final
iv) It sounds like thunder
v) Disobedience is always costly.

There are different forms of audible voices that a lot of God's champions have described in the past.

"And thine ears shall hear a word behind thee, saying this is the way, walk ye in it, when ye turn to the right hand, and when ye turn to the left."

Isaiah 30:21

Types of God's voices

1) Whisper to the ear
2) Hearing a voice behind you
3) Hearing a voice in a crowd
4) Hearing a voice that sounds like that of someone on the first floor speaking to another person on the second floor.
5) Hearing a voice that sounds like that of someone on the second floor speaking to someone on the first floor.

There are other forms but whichever voice you hear must not contradict the Word of God in any way.

Trance and Visions

Trance is the temporary suspension of consciousness that

is experienced when a person is about to see a vision. It usually describes using expressions like "I fell into a trance" or "I saw a vision." Vision could be open or closed.

"He saw a vision evidently about the ninth hour of the day an angel of God coming in to him and saying unto him Cornelius..."

Acts 10:3

An open vision occurs when the person is conscious and alert, while the closed vision occurs while the person is asleep. For closed vision, the person will wake up at the end of the vision and this distinguishes it from dreams.

Angels
This is not very common, but it does occur. It was also more common in the Old Testament than now. God sends His angels to deliver messages to His people. Paul had some angelic visitation:

"For there stood by me this night the angel of the God, whose I am and whom I serve."

Acts 27:23

Dreams
They occur while sleeping. The person could receive a revelation but will not wake up till day break. This is the classic description common to dreams, and it distinguishes it from a closed vision. Dreams were a great way God spoke to Joseph in the Bible (Genesis 37:9).

Circumstances
This method may not be the best but could be important

and even be lifesaving to some people. Balaam could have lost his life to the angel but for his ass that spoke before the prophet's eyes opened (Number 22:21-33). This section was included because of the circumstances surrounding it. Each time I deleted it, my laptop shut down or I lost some of my work. This occurred twice, then I understood that the Lord wanted this section of hearing God's voice to be included. There may be other methods used to hear from God, but these are the main ways. Pay attention to how God speaks to you as a person. A time will come when there will be need to seek God's face for a need you may have, then it will be easy to receive from God.

CHAPTER 5

Influence of Consistency

Consistency refers to the extent of firmness. A champion should be consistent. Consistency is the seed for recognition. It will bring you attention. There is a need to be constant in doing things that will enhance your spiritual inclination. There are three main things champions must consistently do:

1) Studying and meditating on the Word of God because it reveals the culture of God's kingdom and has the ability to transform. It is important that a champion must first of all study to be approved by God. Paul said to Timothy:

"Study to shew thyself approve onto God, a workman that needeth not be ashamed, rightly dividing the word of truth."
2 Timothy 2:15

The Word of God is the uncompromised will of God (Psalm 32:8). It is not limited by any culture or tradition. Champions must strive to do God's will.

"I delight to do thy will, O my God: yea, thy law is within my heart." Psalm 40:8

God is not a respecter of persons. (Galatians 3:28, Act

10:34-35)

"For the Lord your God is God of gods and Lord of lords, a great God, a mighty, and a terrible, which regardeth not persons, nor taketh reward."

Deuteronomy 10:17

Champions cannot but act like God would act and deal with people without partiality.

"But if ye have respect to persons, ye commit sin, and are convinced of the law as transgressors."

James 2:9

The Word of God is absolutely dependable because God cannot lie (Titus 1:2, Number 23:19). God has magnified His Word above His name (Psalms 138:2). The immutability of God's Word verified His nature (Malachi 3:6). The Word of God has integrity, and it will never fail (Psalms 138:2). God watches over His Word to ensure it comes to pass.

"Then said the Lord to me, you have seen well, for I am alert and active, watching over my word to perform it." Jeremiah 1:12 (Amplified version)

- The Word of God is the counsel of God (Psalm 16:7).
- The Word of God cleanses (Ephesians 5:26).
- The Word of God is a mirror (James 1:25).
- The Word of God gives direction (Psalms 119:105).
- The Word of God is pure and gives understanding to the simple (Psalms

12:6 and Psalms 119:130).

Champions do not just believe God's words are true, they act on it. A champion must maintain fellowship with God through constant worship.

"O worship the Lord in the beauty of holiness: fear before him, all the Earth."

Psalm 96:9

Regular worship honors God and invites Him into a relationship. Worship brings God's presence which rubs on the worshipper. It is difficult to be in His presence and not be transformed. There is no champion without an altar and when there is no altar, there is no worship. Every champion must learn to bow his or her knees like the twenty-four elders to worship Him who sits upon the throne (Revelation 5:13-14). Champions need to appear in the presence of God.

"I am the Lord your God, who brought you out of Egypt, out of the land of slavery, "You shall have no other gods before me. "You shall not make for yourself an idol in the form of anything in heaven above or on earth beneath or in the water below. You shall not bow down to them or worship them; for I the Lord your God, am a jealous God, punishing the children for the sin of the fathers to the third and fourth generation of those who hate me, but showing love to a thousand generations of those who love me and keep my commandment." Deuteronomy 5:6-10

It is important that champions learn to worship the Lord in truth and in Spirit as well as offer their bodies as living sacrifices onto the Lord:

"Therefore, I urge you, brothers, in view of God's mercy, to offer

your bodies as living sacrifices, holy and pleasing to God- this is your spiritual act of worship. Do not conform any longer to the pattern of this world, but be transformed but the renewing of your mind. Then you will be able to test and approve what God's will is—his good, pleasing and perfect will." Roman 12:1-2 (NIV)

One way champions renew their strength is in the place of worship. God is the ultimate renewal of strength. Worship with the whole of your heart.

"He gives strength to the weary and increases the power of the weak. Even youths grow tired and weary, and young men stumble and fall; but those who hope in the Lord will renew their strength. They will soar on wings like eagles; they will run and not grow weary, they will walk and not faint." Isaiah 40: 29-31(Message translation)

It is in the place of worship that the exchange of weakness for strength takes place:

"They go from strength to strength; every one of them in Zion appeareth before God."

Psalms 84:7

When champions appear, destinies are changed and lives are transformed. Healings take place in worship. Bitterness, hatred, and anger can be released as you worship the Holy God and pray both in the Holy Ghost and with understanding.

Praying in the Holy Ghost
Champions owe it as a duty to pray in the Holy Ghost. This allows the Spirit of God to help them pray according to the will of God. Thus, all things will work together for good to

them that love God, because the Holy Spirit will help our infirmities to pray in the right direction.

"Likewise the Spirit also helpeth our infirmities: for we know not what we should pray for as we ought: but the Spirit itself maketh intercession for us with groanings which cannot be uttered."

Roman 8:26

The human nature is such that there is enmity between the flesh and the Spirit such that according to Paul, "What I want to do I could not and what I don't want to do, I find myself doing (Roman 7:15). Knowing the Holy Spirit is one of the greatest assets of the champion. Jesus said concerning the Holy Spirit that He will guide us into all truth and will show us things to come (John 16:13). Spending time to pray in the Spirit will draw the champion close to Him.

"Dearly beloveth building up yourself on your most holy faith praying in the Holy Ghost."

Jude 20

I spent a lot of my adolescent years praying in the Holy Ghost. I was consistent in praying sometimes from three hours to 12 hours a day, and the result was a walk through almost all the spiritual gifts with diverse results in ministry. Champions must have a prayer pattern that will be complimentary to enhancing their relationship with God as well as engaging their spiritual growth. Growth is an index of maturity, and Champions must extrapolate and corroborate knowledge from past failures and victory in their walk with God. David, in the battle with Goliath remembered how God was with him when he defended the

sheep against the attack of the lion and the bear. This gave him the boldness as God's avenger, knowing that if God did it one
time, He could do it again. Giving all the glory to God is a champion's way: His glory is exclusively for Him, give it to Him.

Praying with Understanding
Praying with understanding is patterned after the prayer life of Christ. Great men of God maintained their positions through prayer. Jonathan Edward spent 13 hours a day in prayer; John Wesley rises up at 4:00 a.m for prayer even in his eighties. Jesus strategically prayed every now and then. Jesus used the knowledge of the prayer watch to handicap the enemy and paralyze all his activities. Every day has a gate and every season has its gate, so Jesus used the knowledge of the prayer watch to take complete control. No wonder He ruled and reigned during His life.

"Lift up your heads, O ye gates; and be ye lifted up, ye everlasting doors; and the king of glory shall come in. Who is this king of glory? The Lord strong and mighty, the Lord mighty in battle. Lift up your heads, O ye gates; even lift them up, ye everlasting doors; and the king of glory shall come in. Who is this king of glory? The Lord of hosts, he is the king of glory."
Psalm 24:7-10

Jesus had the understanding of the occupants of the gate. The gate is the access to a city. Anyone who takes over the gate controls the events in the city. The elders sit at the gate to make decisions (Proverbs 31:23). Twice, the Lord had to challenge the heads at the gate to grant access. Strategic prayer involves getting to the gate at the right time to take authority. Jesus demonstrated this during his life time by praying at different hours of the day, and this enabled him to deal with the situations the enemy threw at him. Jesus revealed to Peter that the church operating on the knowledge of the keys cannot be dominated upon by the gates of hell (Matthew 16: 16-19). When champions operate based on the knowledge of the prayer watches, there will be results.

The Eight Prayer Watches

1) 6:00 a.m to 9:00 a.m - Time God strengthens believers. Therefore
decree things that they may be established. Cancel every witchcraft and other demonic activities, so they will not prosper in your day. This is the first watch. The Holy Spirit comes during this watch (Acts 2:15).

2) 9:00 a.m to 12 noon - Time for technological scientific breakthroughs and healing of relationships (Matthew 20:3).

3) 12 noon to 3:00 p.m - Time for release of God's promises and exercise of dominion over every attack of the enemy. This is the sixth hour (John 4:6, Acts 26:13).

4) 3:00 p.m to 6:00 p.m - Beginning of the hours of prayer. Time to establish the kingdom of God, and the time the temple veil is torn from top to bottom (Acts 3:1, Matthew 27:45, 46).

5) 6:00 p.m to 9:00 p.m - Time for resurrection, divine judgment, deliverance, and time to deal with issues in economy, as well as educational systems.

6) 9:00 p.m to 12 Midnight - Time for preparation of

visitation. Midnight
represents period of darkness.

7) 12 Midnight to 3:00 a.m - Time to receive the outpouring of grace, time for prayers of protection and destroying limitations.

8) 3:00 a.m to 6:00 a.m - Time for God's intervention, freedom from
satanic activities and to receive blessings from the Lord (womb).

Sometime ago during a series of 40 days fasting, I decided to take over the gate of the day every morning at 5:45 a,m and within a week. we had an outpouring of testimonies. When you take over the gate, you control the day. Uzziah was sixteen years old, when he began to reign. He was noted to be consistent in seeking God in the days of the prophets who had an understanding of the visions of God. His prosperity emerged as a result of his continual seeking of God. The thrice holy God is a prosperous God. You cannot walk with God and be poor. Consistency in his presence always brings prosperity. God always meets every need of his champions.

"And he sought God in the days of Zechariah, who had understanding in the visions of God: and as long as he sought the Lord he prospered." 2 Chronicles 26:5

Consistency is a seed toward prosperity or poverty. What you choose to do or not to do decides your direction toward prosperity or poverty. Some believe tithing is not meant for them while some give tithe and also give offering. The difference lies in their testimonies. Champions understand that tithing is God's way to connect them to the blessing. God doesn't need our money, but we need God; God is the rich.

"For every beast of the forest is mine, and the cattle upon a thousand hills. I know all the fowls of the mountains: and the wild beasts of the field are mine. If I were hungry, I would not tell thee: for the world is mine, and the fullness thereof. Will I eat the flesh of bulls or drink the blood of goats? Offer unto God thanksgiving; and pay thy vows unto the Most high: And call upon me in the day of trouble: I will deliver thee, and thou shalt glorify me."

Psalms 50:10-15

Your tithe and offering should honor God. King Solomon offered thousands of burnt sacrifices to God, and God seeing the heart of Solomon, decided to visit him in the night. He asked Solomon, "What do you want me to do for you?" Champions should see money as a tool for the advancement of the gospel and not as an opportunity to enrich themselves. God knows your need, and that is why the Scripture revealed that:

"For the scripture saith, thou shalt not muzzle the oxen that treadeth out the corn. And the laborer is worthy of his reward." 1 Timothy 5:18

The street of heaven where God dwells is made of gold. Why not stand for the King of Kings and support His gospel with your resources, and the heaven will remain open above you. This is secret of champions.

Cornelius was another man that was a devout gentile who feared God, gave alms to the poor and prayed to God always.

He was consistent in doing these things and subsequently drew the attention of God. The result is the gospel reaching out to the gentiles. Cornelius' name today can never be erased in the history of the gentile believers. What you consistently do will someday place you in God's book of memorial.

"...thy prayers and thine alms are come up for a memorial before God." Act 10:4

Consistency enhances attention. God knows those knees that have never bowed to idols. He knows those that have never compromised and have been consistent in His presence. Repair every broken altar and be consistent in fellowship with God so that your seed will bring you attention before God.

People given to prayers do not spend time in emergency to reach God. I love to pray, and I found trust and solace in God as I have taken the Holy Spirit as my friend. I spent time with Him often, praying in the Holy Ghost sometimes for three hours and up to twelve hours straight. Some years back, my sister sent an urgent message to me that our father was dying. As I cried to God, before my knees could touch the floor, the Holy Spirit spoke to me 'he will not die' and immediately, I started to thank Him instead.

When you spend time with Him, He will recognize you and your voice. Your degree of consistency will release grace that will take you to the throne. It's your turn to be enthroned. You will shine in Jesus name. God revealed the secret to winning in life to Joshua after the death of Moses. Joshua needed to be consistent in meditating on the Word of God to be successful as a leader.

"This book of the law shall not depart out of thy mouth; but thou shall mediate therein day and night, that thou mayest observe to do according to all that is written therein: for then thou shall make thy way prosperous, and then thou shall have good success."

Joshua 1:8

God showed Joshua how consistency can bring success to him, and it helped Joshua to create the path to success; it will help you too. Consistency releases grace that enhances stability, and stability enhances performance. Every champion started out by being stable in their preparation. What you do consistently will soon create the picture that all will see in your life. God does not like lukewarmness. You are either cold or hot. There is nothing like a little to the left and a little to the right. Jesus bitterly complained about the lukewarmness of the church at Laodicea:

"I know thy works, that thou art neither cold nor hot: I would that thou wert cold or hot. So then because thou art lukewarm, and neither cold nor hot, I will spew you out of my mouth."

Revelation 3:15-16

Jesus could help the one that is cold but to the lukewarm, who can help? He dislikes it. It's about time to rekindle the fire and return to your first love. What you will be known for is determined by what you do habitually.

CHAPTER 6

Power of Diligence

Champions are committed to a routine that endorses their release as champions. A dictionary meaning of diligence means a steady effort, assiduity, and persistent application to an undertaking. Diligence has the power to cause a person to stand out among the crowd.

"Seest thou a man diligent in his business? He shall stand before kings; he shall not stand before mean men."

Proverbs 22:29

Diligence will locate and place a person where he belongs. This passage declares where a diligent person can and cannot be found. Diligence will always promote. It will translate a person and plant his feet among kings. Hence, there is need to continue to be diligent in your God-given assignment because the pay day is right at the corner. The God who promotes and sees everywhere and everything even through the darkness of the night will give rewards. It may look like it is not working; just hold on, your lifting is at the door.

"To everything there is a season, and a time to every purpose under Heaven."

Ecclesiastes 3:1

Diligence will yield profit if you do not faint. Diligence ensures where a man will not stand—before mean men. Mean men refers to obscure or unpopular persons. Diligence takes a man from among unpopular people and places him among the people that matter—kings and nobles. A diligent person can only be delayed but not stopped. Diligence is a quiet way to rise to the top. You will rise in Jesus name. The Champion will emerge if he is diligent in spiritual things. Joseph, the beloved son of Jacob was an example of a diligent man who excelled at everything he laid his hands on starting from his father's house, where his quality was noticed by his father. In the house of Potiphar, he was in charge of everything his master had but his wife. In Pharaoh's jail, he was in charge of the prisoners. God loves diligent people, hence they prosper.

"But the Lord was with Joseph, and shewed him mercy, and gave him favor in the sight of the keeper of the prison."

Genesis 39:21

Diligence always attracts the favor of the owner of the business. Whatsoever work the hand of a diligent person finds, he always does it as onto the Lord. The diligent employee is that person the boss will not need to sweat over because he does not need supervision.

"Go to the ant, thou sluggard; consider her ways and be wise: which having no guide, over seer, or ruler, provideth her meat in the summer, and gathereth her food in the harvest."

Proverbs 6:6-8

The ants demonstrate the ability to work and do the right

thing at the right time, yet they don't have a guide. They are well coordinated in their assignment, thus they have meat to eat in due season. The diligent person works as if he owns the business. Diligent people have the feeling of the eye of God watching everything they do. The fear of God is evident in their work and most of the time, they end up being best employees of a business.

"He becometh poor that dealeth with a slack hand: but the hand of the diligent maketh rich." Proverbs 10:4

Diligence promotes and exposes a champion. A diligent man never lacks good things.

"Wherefore the rather, brethren, give diligence to make your calling and election sure: for if ye do these things, ye shall never fall: For so an entrance shall be ministered unto you abundantly into everlasting kingdom of our Lord and Savior Jesus Christ." 2 Peter 1:10-12

Diligence allows a champion access to greatness. What you choose to honor determines the door you will access. When champions honor Jesus Christ, doors of abundance in the kingdom of Christ are opened on to them. Jesus Christ is the only door to eternal life.

"Jesus saith on to them I am the way, the truth and the life. No man cometh on to the father but by me."

John 14:6

Every one that accepts Christ into his or her life has access to the Father as well as eternal life.

The Passion of Champions

Champions have passion for the things of the kingdom of God. They support the gospel with their resources, and their hearts are sold out to the things of God. Their words are their bonds. Champions battle daily to overcome the conflict between the Spirit and the flesh, so they walk in the Spirit without fulfilling the desires of the flesh (Galatians 5:16).

1) They are dependable and can be counted upon by God at any time for any assignment. Champions don't see themselves as too big for any assignment.
2) Pride and arrogance are abominations to them.
3) Works of the flesh have no place in their lives (Galatians 5:19-21).
4) Humility is their watchword.
5) Service to God is their way of life
6) God's love (Agape) fills their hearts (1 Corinthians 13:1-13).
7) The gifts of the Holy Spirit are eminent in their lives (1 Corinthians 12). Champions desire and covet the best gifts.

CHAPTER 7

Influence of Connection

To be a champion, you must be connected to God. A champion is simply a vessel to demonstrate the glory of God.

"If thou faint in the day of adversary, thy strength is small." Proverbs 24:12

A connected man never lacks any need. Show me a champion who never loses a battle, and I will show you a person who has never abandoned his source. Your connection answers for you during adversity. One of the unparalleled secrets of champions is their connection to their source.

"Nevertheless I have somewhat against thee, because thou hast left thy first love." Revelation 2:4

"For my people have committed two evils; they have forsaken me the fountain of living waters, and hewed them out cisterns, broken cisterns, that can hold no water."

Jeremiah 2:13

Every time Israel turns away from God, their enemies plunder and impoverish them. When the champion is disconnected from the source, he dries up. Check yourself, are you still connected to the source?

"And he shall be like a tree planted by the rivers of water, that bringeth forth his fruit in his season; his leaf also shall not wither; and whatsoever he doeth shall prosper."

Psalms 1:3

Jesus is inviting you today to come and drink. Get connected to the rivers of living water that is ever flowing. Jesus wants you connected to the Holy Spirit:

"In the last day, that great day of the feast, Jesus stood and cried, saying, if any man thirsts, let him come and drink. He that believeth on me, as the scripture hath said, out of his belly shall flow rivers of living water." John 7: 37-38

God's Champions can't reign alone without the Holy Spirit, and they don't mess with their fellowship with God. They jealously guard it to make sure nothing hinders the relationship. The Most high never abandons any project. God wants to have a relationship with every one created in his image. You can enter into this relationship today by simply asking Jesus to come into your life, be your Lord and savior and cleanse you of every past sin. If you prayed that prayer, you just got born again and reconnected to God. The next thing is to make sure to join a Bible-believing and Holy Spirit-filled church.

"I was glad when they said unto me, let us go into the house of the Lord." Psalms 122:1

The connection to God through the Holy Spirit provides access to unending supplies of God's assistance.

The Holy Spirit as the Source of Connection

The champion is never isolated, rather he is connected to the ever flowing grace of God through the Holy Spirit. Jesus made it clear to his disciples how important the role of the Holy Spirit is in the life of the believer.

"Nevertheless I tell you the truth: it is expedient for you that I go away, the comforter will not come unto you; but if I go not away, the comforter will not unto you; but if I depart, I will send him unto you."

John 16:7

From this Scripture, it is clear that a believer needs the Holy Spirit more than ever. If Jesus needed Him to overcome, then it is imperative that believers experience His role in their lives.

"How God anointed Jesus of Nazareth with the Holy Ghost and with power: who went about doing good, and healing all that were oppressed of the devil; for God was with him."

Act 10:38

Jesus our greatest iconic champion excelled by the help of the Holy Spirit. You need Him more than any other thing in this world. The Holy Spirit should be your best friend, a companion through life. The Holy Spirit is God's positional system (GPS) that will help you navigate your path to destiny.

Many are experiencing rough terrains and are locked up in life's wilderness for lack of knowledge of the Holy Spirit. Some only know the letters but have never had an opportunity of meeting Him, but your case is different. You don't have to fast and pray or wait in the upper room anymore. He is here. You can meet Him now if you will invite Him into your life. The Holy Spirit will be your guide in all things. He will help you understand the Bible He wrote (2 Timothy 3:16). When you wake up startled by bad dreams and burdens in the middle of the night and don't know what to do, He will be right there to help you to pray (Roman 8:26). The Holy Spirit is the spirit of champions. Champions depend on Him to win. You need Him to make a difference in your generation.

"For God has not given us the spirit of fear; but of power, and of love, and of a sound mind."

2 Timothy 1:7

The Holy Spirit is the spirit of boldness that distinguishes champions. He was upon David and made him unintimidated by Goliath's status and resume of warfare experience.

"And David spake to the men that stood by him, saying, what shall be done to the man that killeth this Philistine, and taketh away the reproach from Israel? For who is this uncircumcised Philistine, that he should defy the armies of the living God."

1 Samuel 17:26

Champions are defenders of God. David was infuriated by the words Goliath was verbalizing. He could not comprehend what audacity an infidel had to intimidate the army of the living God. He was ready to diffuse the tension and change the tide. Champions are tide changers; they change the altitude and create the atmosphere of faith for God to intervene.

"That your faith should not stand in the wisdom of men, but in

the power of God."

1 Corinthians 2:5

The arm of flesh will fail. Only God never fails if you trust in Him. Even Jesus constantly and continuously prayed to the Father because He trusted in Him. If you trust in God, He will never disappoint you.

CHAPTER 8

Language of a Champion

Champions have a language and for anyone to be a champion, it is imperative that he or she speaks like one. Language allows and enhances communication, and communication enables understanding, and understanding enhances relationships. A well communicated language gets appropriate responses. Without proper use of right words, an expected response cannot be provoked. Every champion must learn kingdom language. The kingdom language is independent of the events in the "seen realm".

"(As it is written, I HAVE MADE THEE A FATHER OF MANY NATIONS,) before him whom he believed, even God who quickeneth the death and calleth those things that be not as though they were."

Roman 4:17

It is the culture of the kingdom to call out of the unseen realm those things you expect to see in the seen realm. Therefore, it is only traditional in the kingdom for the weak to say I'm strong and the sick to say I'm healed, and those things cannot but be as they have been spoken. Speak it right, and you will see it manifest out right.

When the champion speaks victory, it's only normal in the supernatural realm for those things that are supernatural to be experienced in the natural realm as common experience.

To the champion, the things the world refers to as supernatural are normal ways of life. Speak it right, and you will see it manifest out right. Former world heavy weight champion Mike Tyson was defeated by a challenger Evander Holyfield who understands the language of champions. He came into the ring with a proof of what he had been speaking to himself, written boldly on his shirt. And, he left the ring with the title of champion. He came with the words and sat on the throne as the heavy weight champion of the world. Champions have language; start speaking it right, today.

"Through faith we understand that the world were framed by the Word of God, so that things which are seen were not of things which do appear." Hebrew 11:3

Let your words frame your world. Champions make clear sounds. David declared unto Saul the king of Israel by connecting his past victories over the lion and the bear to God's providence.

"David said moreover, the Lord that delivered me out of the paw of the lion, and out of the paw of the bear, he will deliver me out of the hand of this Philistine. And Saul said unto David, go, and the Lord be with thee." 1 Samuel 17:37

David firmly and clearly described what Goliath should expect for defiling the army of the living God and reproaching His name.

"Then said David unto the Philistine, thou cometh to me with a sword, and with a spear, and with a shield: but I come to thee in the name of the Lord of host, the God of the armies of Israel, whom thou hast defiled. This day will the Lord deliver thee into my hand: and I will spite thee, and take thine head from thee; and I will give the carcasses of the host of the Philistine this day unto the fowl of the air, and to the wild beasts of the earth; that all the earth may know that there is a God in Israel. And all this assembly shall know that the Lord saveth not with sword and spear: for the battle is the Lord's and he will give you into our hands." 1 Samuel 17:45-47

David connected God with the battle, telling Him that He should take the battle as His own, because He is their God. His name was being reproached, and it was an opportunity to show off by bringing victory with an inferior weapon to the sword, spear, and shield. David invoked the name of Jehovah who fights battle "The Lord of Host", and the Lord of Host showed up and gave him the victory. Every time a person connects God with a situation and invokes the name of the Lord into the "situation", God is bound to be interested in the case. King Hezekiah is another example when king Sennacherib of Assyria besieged Judah. King Sennacherib sent his servants with words of intimidation that could cause anyone without God to develop chills to the core of their bones. He painted the resume of success of the king of Assyria and his army. In fact, it was really intimidating.

"Hath any of the gods of the nations delivered at all his land out of the hand of the king of Assyria? Where are the gods of Hamath, and of Arpad? Where are the gods of Sepharvaim, Hena, and Ivah? Have they delivered Samaria out of mine

hand? Who are they among all the gods of the countries that have delivered their country out of mine hand, that the Lord should deliver Jerusalem out of mine hand?"

2 King 18:33-35

After hearing these words from the servant of the king of Assyria, the king of Israel rent his cloth. King Hezekiah knew champions do have troubles and challenges that may be bigger than what they can handle, so he declared in a message to the prophet Amos in 2 King 19:3-4:

"And they said unto him, thus saith Hezekiah, this day is a day of trouble, and of rebuke, and of blasphemy: for the children are come to the birth, and there is not strength to bring forth. It may be the Lord thy God will hear all the words of Rabshakeh, whom the king of Assyria his master hath sent to reproach the living God; and will reprove the words which the Lord thy God hath heard; wherefore lift up thy prayer for the remnant that are left."

There is no champion without battles. Every champion faces battles. The outcome of the battle is determined by who you went into the battle with. Is it your strength, satanic powers or the Lord of Host? Champions always go with the Lord of Host; thus they never lose any battle.

"Some trust in chariots, some in horses but we will remember the name of the Lord our God."

Psalm 20:7

King Sennacherib of Assyria thought that because he defeated Israel and took over Samaria, he could do the same over Judah and take over Jerusalem. It is easy to know why King Sennacherib was successful over Samaria:

"And the king of Assyria did carry away Israel unto Assyria, and put them in Halah and in Habor by the river of Gozan, and in the cities of Medes" Because they obeyed not the voice of the Lord their God, but transgressed His covenant, and all that Moses the servant of the Lord commanded, and would not hear them, nor do them." 2 Kings 18:11-12

When champions decide to do things their way, they get enslaved and their enemies laugh over them. Champions are mindful of their association, because it affects their choices in life.

"Blessed is the man that walketh not in the counsel of the ungodly, nor standeth in the way of sinners, nor sit in the seat of scornful." Psalm 1:1

You cannot walk in wrong counsel or hang around wrong companies and expect things to work out right. Champions carefully choose who to associate with. Who you choose as your friend determines your altitude in life. A wrong association is a strong influence towards a wrong direction and unaccomplished destiny. Your victory is only guaranteed, if you are in partnership with the Lord of Host. Choose rightly. Your choice is an index of your direction to your posterity. Choose wisely.

"And it came to pass, when Joshua was by Jericho, that he lifted up his eyes and looked, and, behold, there stood a man over against him with his sword drawn in his hand: and Joshua went unto him, and said unto him, Art thou for us, or for our adversaries? And he said, nay; but as captain of the host of the Lord am I now come. And Joshua fell on his face to the earth, and did worship, and said unto him, what saith my Lord unto

his servant?" Joshua 5:13-14

With the walls of Jericho constituting an obstruction to advancement to the promise land, Joshua was obviously out of options and strategies to conquer Jericho as the city was shut down because of the children of Israel. The situation was virtually hopeless, and Joshua was clueless about what next to do. Champions always wait on God before making a move. I remember a couple of years back when I bought a business valued at $140,000. I thought that because God was quiet, it meant a go-ahead. Little did I know that it was a well packaged scam that would cost me several thousands of dollars, heart ache, and waste of my time. The previous owner lied about everything and landed me close to bankruptcy. I learned a very bitter lesson.

In 1 Samuel 13:8-12, King Saul was supposed to wait for Prophet Samuel but after the prophet did not arrive on time, Saul decided "Hey, bring the sheep and the knife, the job of Prophet Samuel is easy, I used to slaughter sheep for my father when I was at home." (Paraphrased) And, Saul went ahead to offer burnt offerings to God. Consequently, Saul lost his throne that day. In the name of Jesus, everything and anything that wants to dethrone you prematurely will not prosper. I have come to learn to move only when the cloud of glory changes position. Never let anyone hurry you into making a decision you are not sure of. Champions always inquire of the Lord, should I pursue? Will you deliver them into my hands?

"Ask and it shall be given you; seek, and ye shall find; knock, and it shall be opened unto you: For everyone that asketh receiveth; and he that seeketh findeth; and to him that

knocketh it shall be opened." Matthew 7:7-8

Joshua chose to ask the captain of the Lord of host what He will want him to do. What will you do when the captain of the host of the Lord shows up? Will you ignore Him or worship Him? Your choice will certainly decide the outcome. You will laugh last over every life situation in Jesus precious name. As long you walk with Him, you will never taste defeat. The choice is yours, choose and speak wisely. What you say is what you see. If you want to see good things, speak the right words.

Words create and if you say them long enough, you will get what you say. Decide what you want and let what you want align with what you say. Words either create or destroy. Let your words be creative. Some parents use common curse words on their children every now and then. Later in the future, when the child starts to act crazy, they begin to wonder what is wrong with the child. A couple of months ago, my family was in the market for a property. We went everywhere in search of the house God has shown us for months. I was not aware that the agent taking me around was taking note of my words. Irrespective of whether we received a good or bad news about the properties we were checking, my response was always "It is well". For 90 days, all that came out of my lips was "It is well". While the banking process was taking longer than anticipated because the property was bank owned and nobody knew what the outcome will be; whether the bank will accept our offer or not, my confession was still "It is well". When it was 90 days, I saw in a vision the property which the Lord chose for us and it was possible for us to close the deal. Couple of weeks after, the agent called me and told me those words inspired him to go and procure a land and build his own house too.

"But what saith it? The word is nigh thee, even in the mouth, and in thy heart: that is, the word of faith, which we preach." Romans 10:8

Say it loud and clear. Declare your heart desire, print it on a paper and look at it over and over again, talk about it to friends, meditate on it in the evening, pray about it and keep on waiting as you confess your desire into the physical realm. This is the champion way. In the mid-1990s, I was returning in company of a friend then to the medical campus when it started to rain. Three thoughts came into my mind, first was to keep walking and get wet or to run and avoid the rain. I also thought that young believers would see the teachers of faith of the campus running, then a third thought interjected saying, "why not stop the rain." I thought that to stop the rain was a cool idea and faith rose up within me. I suddenly clapped my hands and screamed out "rain stop now" and to my amazement, the rain was immediately suspended on us while falling some six foot away from us.

Champions Cannot Walk in Disobedience
For a champion to reign for a long time there is need to heed to divine instructions. Disobedience is rebellion in process, and it's like the sin of witchcraft. Someone once said anything that has two heads is a monster. You cannot serve two masters. Instructions are received from the Lord and are important for a champion to finish well. When there is displaced loyalty, a champion may suffer setbacks.

"And Samuel said, Hath the Lord great delight in burnt

offerings and sacrifices, as in obeying the voice of the Lord? Behold to obey is better than sacrifice, and to hearken than the fat of rams. For rebellion is as the sin of witchcraft, and stubbornness is as iniquity and idolatry. Because thou hast rejected the word of the Lord, he hath also rejected thee from being king." 1 Samuel 15:22-23

King Saul had just been enthroned by the prophet, when he suddenly lost his focus. He became interested in pleasing the people rather than God who appointed him. God the appointer backed off at that time. When a champion loses the backing of the appointer, the journey becomes fruitless and it becomes showmanship. It's only a matter of time before it comes to an end. I have always cherished the presence of the Holy Spirit; to lose Him is to embark on a journey to "nowhere". The kingdom of Saul had barely been established by God before it was deleted.

"And Samuel said on to Saul, Thou hast done foolishly: thou hast not kept the commandment of the Lord thy God, which he commanded thee: for now would the Lord have established thy kingdom upon Israel forever. But now thy kingdom shall not continue: the Lord hath sought him a man after his own heart, and the Lord hath commanded him to be captain over his people, because thou hast not kept that which the Lord commanded thee." 1 Samuel 13:13-14

Champions depend solely on the Most high God and therefore they last. Their sufficiency is of the Lord, and He will meet all their needs.

"It is a terrible thing to fall into the hand of God." Hebrew 10:31

Remember, Achan who took of the accursed things from the camp of the enemy, and he contaminated the whole Israel by bringing them into disobedience. The result was Israel running away from their enemy (Joshua 7).

CONCLUSION

In conclusion, God created you in his own image, and He has a plan and purpose for your life. A lot of champions have died without achieving the plan of God for them. A lot of gifts have been left undiscovered and unused, and statistics are increasing by the day. It's about time the champion in you arose to fulfill your destiny in your generation. Behold, God and your generation is waiting for your manifestation.

"For the earnest expectation of the creation waiteth for the manifestation of the sons of God."

Roman 8:19

Remember, you are not from here. Your kingdom has a language and if you must succeed, you need to speak the kingdom language to get the kingdom's results. Take heed unto yourself and remember at all times how you have believed and received the gospel. Buckle down and join the chariot; you can shine as the Lord's champion.

Prayers
• Every seed of champions will begin to grow in my life today in Jesus name.
• I destroy every satanic yoke in my life, hidden or revealed in Jesus name.
• I command every oppression and satanic harassment to

stop now in the name of Jesus.

• I rebuke the spirit of hypocrisy, deceit and all lying spirits. I command you to cease operation against me in Jesus name.

• My Father, My Father, My Father, anywhere my name is mentioned for evil, or any group of people mentioning my name for evil, let your thunder strike them dead in Jesus name.

• Every monitoring agent over my life, I command the arrows of the Lord to destroy you now in Jesus name.

• I am a champion, and I must be victorious. Any power swallowing my destiny, vomit it now by fire in Jesus name.

• In the name of Jesus, I call out my destiny from anywhere it is hidden now.

• I decree that any association that is not fostering godliness in my life be destroyed today by fire in Jesus name.

• I break up every ungodly relationship; spiritually and physically by the blood of Jesus.

• I neutralize and counteract every effect of strange and ungodly association in my life, with the blood of Jesus.

• Every destiny swapping power, be destroyed now in Jesus name.

• I pray that the Holy Spirit helps me to control my appetite. Whatsoever is not good for my body, soul, and spirit I will not desire in Jesus name.

• I rebuke every spirit of barrenness in my life: spiritually, financially, physically and materially in Jesus name.

• I break every demonic covenant operating in my life in Jesus name.

• I pray for grace to recover everything the devil has stolen from me, and my family in Jesus name.

• I break every circle of failure, and I begin to make progress now in Jesus name.

• I must emerge as a champion therefore I will not die before my time. Every spirit of death returns to sender now in Jesus name.

• Everything that does not want me to enter into my greatness, I command you to be paralyzed now in Jesus name.

ABOUT THE AUTHOR

Olukayode Agbeyomi

Bishop (Dr.) Kayode Agbeyomi is the President and Founder of Global Empowerment Christian Center, Georgia, USA. He is an Apostle by calling and is anointed for signs and wonders. He has ministered within and outside the United States of America, and his ministry to the body of Christ involves restoring health and good life through healing, prophetic deliverance, and the prosperity anointing. He is sent to raise a mighty army through the teaching of the Word of God and operations of the power gifts. A medical doctor by profession, he happily married to Feyi and they are blessed with three sons: Glory, David and Toyan.